JUNIOR
BIOGRAPHIES

MEGHAN
MARKLE

AMERICAN ROYAL

Enslow Publishing
101 W. 23rd Street
Suite 240
New York, NY 10011
USA
enslow.com

Elizabeth Krajnik

advocate A person who argues for or supports an idea or plan.

calligraphy Beautiful artistic handwriting.

charity An organization or fund for helping the needy.

defamation The act of saying false things in order to make people have a bad opinion of someone or something.

ethnicity One's racial, national, tribal, religious, linguistic, or cultural origin or background.

gender The state of being male or female.

interracial Involving people of different races.

paralegal A person whose job is to assist a lawyer.

racist Showing or feeling that one group or race of people is better than another group or race.

sexist Showing or feeling that one sex is better than the other.

CONTENTS

Meghan Markle

CHAPTER 1

GROWING UP IN HOLLYWOOD

American actress Meghan Markle started acting in 2002. She didn't catch her big break until 2011, when she landed her starring role as Rachel Zane on the TV show *Suits.* Markle has also had roles in big movies such as *Horrible Bosses.* Today, Meghan is getting ready to marry her real-life prince, Prince Harry of Great Britain, and challenging the standards of modern-day royalty.

A STAR IS BORN

Rachel Meghan Markle was born on August 4, 1981. Her father, Thomas Markle, is an award-winning television lighting director, and her mother, Doria Ragland, is a yoga instructor and social worker. Thomas Markle is

Meghan Markle convinced a dish soap company to change a sexist TV commercial when she was just 11 years old.

Meghan and Prince Harry take part in **charity** events to raise awareness for medical conditions such as AIDS.

Caucasian, and Doria Ragland is African American. The two divorced in 1988. Meghan has two older half-siblings, Thomas Markle Junior and Samantha Grant, from her father's first marriage.

Meghan went to Hollywood

Meghan Says:

"With fame comes opportunity, but in my opinion, it also includes responsibility—to **advocate** and share, to focus less on glass slippers and more on pushing through glass ceilings, and if I'm lucky enough—then to inspire."

Little Red Schoolhouse. While there, she noticed that a TV commercial for dish soap suggested that women's roles were only in the home. Meghan didn't agree with the message the commercial was sending. She wrote a letter to a number of people in power, including Hillary Clinton, who was first lady of the United States at the time.

Meghan and her mother, Doria (*pictured left*), attended the 2017 Invictus Games in Toronto, Canada.

CHAPTER 2
MAKING IT BIG

Before Meghan became famous, she grew up like most other teenagers. She attended Immaculate Heart High School, an all-girls Catholic private school in Los Angeles, California. After high school, Meghan studied theater and international studies at Northwestern University in Illinois and graduated in 2003.

In 2002, Meghan landed her first TV acting role as an extra in one episode of *General Hospital*. During her senior year of college, Meghan worked at the US Embassy in Argentina. To make money while trying out for different roles, Meghan appeared on a game show called *Deal or No Deal*. Even though this TV show was a paid job, it taught Meghan which types of acting she wanted to be

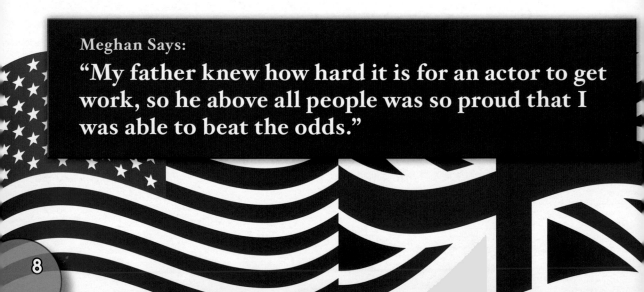

Meghan Says:

"My father knew how hard it is for an actor to get work, so he above all people was so proud that I was able to beat the odds."

Meghan appeared on four episodes of *Deal or No Deal* in 2007.

On October 11, 2011, Meghan attended the Anti-**Defamation** League Industry Awards dinner.

doing instead. Meghan also did **calligraphy** on the side to make extra money to support herself while looking for acting work.

Early in her career, Meghan had small guest roles on TV shows including *CSI: NY*; *CSI: Miami*; and *90210*.

In 2010, Meghan landed her big break. She was chosen to play the role of Rachel Zane, a **paralegal**, on the TV show *Suits*. Eventually, Meghan's character becomes a lawyer. Meghan left the show after filming for the seventh season ended in late 2017.

The pilot, or first episode, of *Suits* aired on June 23, 2011.

On September 10, 2011, Meghan married Trevor Engelson, a Hollywood agent and producer, in Ocho Rios, Jamaica. The couple had been dating since 2004. Meghan even has a cameo in one of the movies Trevor produced!

Many of Meghan's personality traits, including her sense of humor and ambition, were used to create Rachel Zane's character.

It is called *Remember Me* and it stars Robert Pattinson, the lead in the Twilight movies. A few months before getting married, Meghan landed her role on *Suits*. She lived in Toronto, Canada, while the show was being filmed. Trevor lived in Los Angeles. In August 2013, Meghan and Trevor decided to get divorced.

Chapter 3
Fighting for Equality

From a young age, Meghan has had to fight to be treated as an equal. When she was in seventh grade, Meghan wasn't sure which box to check for her **ethnicity**: black or Caucasian. A teacher told her she looked Caucasian and that she should check the box for Caucasian. Her father told her that the next time she had to do that, she should draw her own box.

In college, one of the girls living in Meghan's residence hall implied that Meghan's parents were divorced because they were an **interracial** couple.

As a biracial actress, finding acting work was often difficult for Meghan. Roles come with character descriptions, many of which are very specific. Meghan often found that even when she could change her

Meghan found her match in the role of Rachel Zane. The producers weren't looking for a specific type of person, just the perfect Rachel.

Meghan named her blog *The Tig* after her favorite wine: Tignanello.

appearance to fit a role, she wasn't white enough or black enough. Even though Meghan was proud the producers chose her for the role in *Suits,* many of the show's fans weren't. People tweeted **racist** things about Meghan. The things those people said hurt her. It took time for her to heal. Today, Meghan embraces her ethnicity.

In 2014, Meghan created a lifestyle blog named *The Tig* where she could discuss topics ranging from food,

On March 10, 2015, Meghan attended the Step It Up for Gender Equality celebration in New York City.

Meghan Says:

"You don't have to play dress up to be a feminist. You are a feminist exactly the way you are . . . There's no uniform for feminism."

to travel, to fashion, to beauty. Meghan used her blog to discuss issues that come up in many people's lives, such as feeling comfortable in your own skin. After writing a blog about self-worth on Independence Day, Meghan was contacted by the United Nations (UN). On a one-week break from filming *Suits*, she interned at UN headquarters. This was the start of a new journey for Meghan in women's advocacy.

CHAPTER 4
AN ACTIVIST AND A PRINCESS

Partnering with the UN is just one way Meghan has used her voice for good. In 2015, the UN named Meghan a UN Women's **advocate** for political participation and leadership. On March 10, 2015, she gave a speech in which she discussed her background in women's advocacy and the need for **gender** equality in all parts of life— especially in politics.

Meghan has attended a number of events to show her support for causes she cares about. In 2015, she attended the Dove Self-Esteem Project event in Toronto, Canada. The project's goal is to help young people reach their full potential by boosting their self-esteem.

In 2016, Meghan went to Rwanda as a global ambassador with World Vision Canada to educate children on the importance of clean water.

Meghan's mom went with her to the UN Women's 20th Anniversary of the Fourth World Conference of Women in Beijing.

Meghan also traveled to India with World Vision to talk about issues young girls and women in the country have to deal with, such as education, hygiene, and health care.

Meghan's compassion got the attention of one very special person. In July 2016, Meghan's friend set her up on a date with Prince Harry Windsor of Great Britain! Drawn to Meghan's kindness, Harry fell in love and defended her against racist remarks from the public. In November 2017, Harry proposed and the world buzzed about the new royal engagement—and the new American princess.

At the Dove Self-Esteem Project event, Meghan talked about her own struggles with self-esteem when she was younger.

Meghan Says:

"In doing this, we remind girls that their small voices are, in fact, not small at all and that they can effect change. In doing this, we remind women that their involvement matters . . ."

All of Meghan's activist work has set her apart from many of the British princesses that have come before her. Taking up humanitarian work is part of the princess life, but Meghan has already found causes she's passionate about.

Even though she will no longer be an actress, Meghan will continue to fight for equality and social change. She wants to focus her efforts on charitable causes in the UK and British Commonwealth. Meghan Markle will be a new kind of princess.

TIMELINE

August 4, 1981 Rachel Meghan Markle is born.

2002 Meghan gets her first acting job on the TV show *General Hospital.*

2003 Meghan graduates from Northwestern University.

July 2011 Meghan is cast as Rachel Zane on the TV show *Suits.*

September 10, 2011 Meghan marries Trevor Engelson.

August 2013 Meghan and Trevor get divorced.

2014 Meghan begins working on her lifestyle blog, *The Tig.*

March 10, 2015 Meghan gives a speech on women's equality as a UN Women's advocate for political participation and leadership.

June 2016 Meghan begins dating Prince Harry of Britain.

November 27, 2017 Meghan and Prince Harry announce their engagement.

January 2018 Meghan deletes all her social media.

May 19, 2018 Meghan and Prince Harry are set to marry.

LEARN MORE

Books

Carroll, Leslie. *American Princess: The Love Story of Meghan Markle and Prince Harry.* New York, NY: William Morrow Paperbacks, 2018.

Junor, Penny. *Prince Harry: Brother, Soldier, Son.* New York, NY: Grand Central Publishing, 2014.

Sadat, Halima. *Harry & Meghan: A Royal Engagement.* London, UK: Pavilion, 2018.

Websites

Prince Henry of Wales
www.princehenryofwales.org
Learn more about Prince Harry's life and the causes he supports.

The Royal Family
www.royal.uk/royal-family
Keep up to date on news about Meghan Markle and Prince Harry.

INDEX

Published in 2019 by Enslow Publishing, LLC.
101 W. 23rd Street, Suite 240, New York, NY 10011

Cataloging-in-Publication Data

Name: Krajnik, Elizabeth.
Title: Meghan Markle: American royal / Elizabeth Krajnik.
Description: New York : Enslow Publishing, 2019. | Series: Junior biographies | Includes bibliographic references and index. | Audience: Grades 3-6.
Identifiers: ISBN 9781978505896 (pbk.) | ISBN 9781978505919 (library bound) | 9781978505902 (6 pack)
Subjects: LCSH: Markle, Meghan, 1981- —Juvenile literature. | Television actors and actresses—United States—Biography—Juvenile literature. | Princesses—Great Britain—Biography—Juvenile literature.
Classification: LCC PN2287.M375 K73 2019 | DDC 791.4502/8092 B—dc23

To Our Readers: We have done our best to make sure all website addresses in this book were active and appropriate when we went to press. However, the author and the publisher have no control over and assume no liability for the material available on those websites or on any websites they may link to. Any comments or suggestions can be sent by email to customerservice@enslow.com.

Photo Credits: Cover, p. 1 Karwai Tang/WireImage/Getty Images; p. 4 Karwai Tang/WireImage/Getty Images; p. 6 WPA Pool/Getty Images; p. 7 Geoff Robins/AFP/Getty Images; p. 9 Amy Tierney/WireImage/Getty Images; p. 10 Michael Tran/FilmMagic/Getty Images; p. 11 Frederick M. Brown/Getty Images; p. 14 Michael Tullberg/Getty Images; p. 16 Esther Horvath/FilmMagic/Getty Images; p. 19 Sylvain Gaboury/Patrick McMullan/Getty Images; p. 20 George Pimentel/WireImage/Getty Images; back cover, pp. 2, 3, 22, 23, 24 (curves graphic) Alena Kazlouskaya/Shutterstock.com; interior page bottoms (American and British flags) Mila Duchinskaya/Shutterstock.com.